Published by Creative Education
P.O. Box 227, Mankato, Minnesota 56002
Creative Education is an imprint of The Creative Company

Design and production by Blue Design
Printed in the United States of America

Photographs by Corbis (Bettmann), Getty Images (Brian Bahr, Al Bello, Jonathan Daniel, John Grieshop/MLB Photos, Brad Mangin/MLB Photos, Francis Miller//Time Life Pictures, National Baseball Hall of Fame Library/MLB Photos, Rich Pilling/MLB Photos, Robert Riger Collection, Mark Rucker/Transcendental Graphics, Donald F. Smith//Time Life Pictures, Three Lions, Ron Vesely/MLB Photos)

Library of Congress Cataloging-in-Publication Data

O'Hearn, Michael, 1972-
The story of the Chicago White Sox / by Michael O'Hearn.
p. cm. — (Baseball: the great American game)
Includes index.
ISBN-13: 978-1-58341-483-5
1. Chicago White Sox (Baseball team)—History—Juvenile literature. I. Title. II. Series.

GV875.C58O44 2007
796.357'640977311—dc22   2006029815

First Edition
9 8 7 6 5 4 3 2 1

Cover: Outfielder Jermaine Dye
Page 1: Second baseman Geoff Blum
Page 3: First baseman Paul Konerko

THE STORY OF THE

CHICAGO
WHITE SOX

by Michael O'Hara

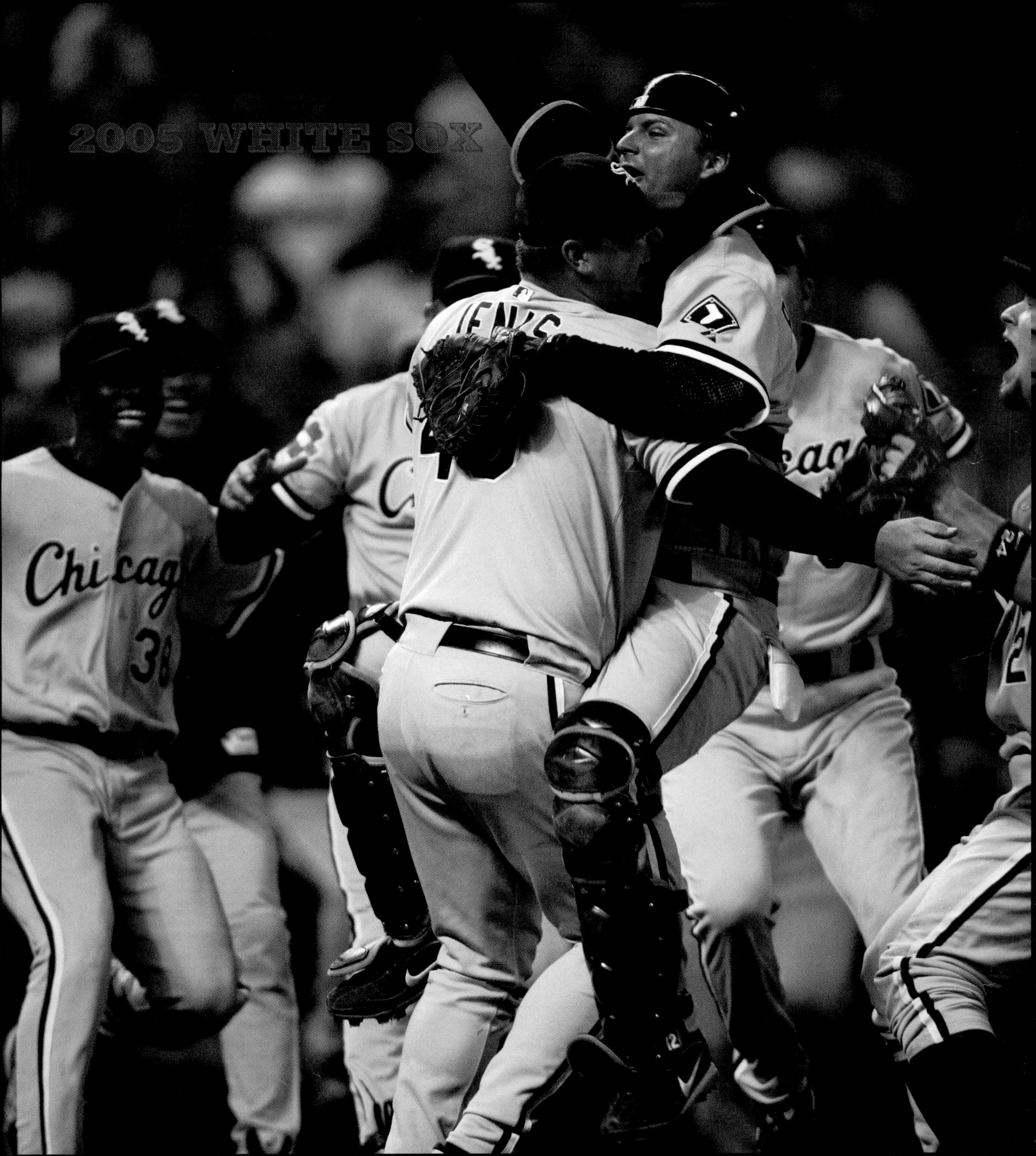
2005 WHITE SOX
Chicago
38

THE STORY OF THE
Chicago White Sox

The Chicago White Sox lead the Houston Astros three games to none in the 2005 World Series, but it's no rout; the series' first three games have each been decided by two runs or fewer. Now, in the eighth inning of a scoreless Game 4, with pinch hitter Willie Harris on third base, Chicago outfielder Jermaine Dye has a chance to put the final nail in the Astros' coffin. He steps into the batter's box and stares out at Houston's Brad Lidge, a tough closer with a nasty fastball. Lidge delivers a first-pitch fireball, and Dye whiffs at it. But when the next pitch arrives, Dye connects, smacking the ball into the dirt and through the infield, past the outstretched glove of Astros shortstop Adam Everett. Harris charges home to eke out the only run of the game. An inning later, the celebration begins—Chicago has its first world championship in 88 years.

BUILDING AND BURNING

In 1871, Chicago burned. The Great Chicago Fire started in a barn and spread through the city's center for two days until rain finally halted the blaze. The fire killed 300 people, left another 100,000 homeless, and caused more than $200 million in damage. The midwestern metropolis, which was built on the iron, steel, and meatpacking industries, was quickly rebuilt, but many residents moved south, away from the city's center. In time, a mix of immigrant populations—Irish, Scottish, Welsh, German, and Polish—made their homes in Chicago's south side. It was in this working-class area of Chicago that baseball player-turned-owner Charlie Comiskey made a home for a franchise that came to be known as the White Sox.

In 1900, Comiskey moved his minor-league franchise from St. Paul, Minnesota, to Chicago to join the new American League (AL). Chicago's "White Stockings," along with teams in Milwaukee, Minneapolis, Indianapolis, Kansas City, Detroit, Cleve-

CHARLIE COMISKEY – Comiskey's first experiences in pro baseball were as a first baseman and manager for the St. Louis Browns in the 1880s. He later purchased the Sioux City (Iowa) White Stockings and moved them to St. Paul and then Chicago.

CHICAGO

America's third-biggest city, Chicago is famous for its winds, great skyscrapers, and deep-rooted sports traditions.

THE TRIBUNE ALWAYS MAKES A HIT WITH ITS SPORTIN

THE HITLESS WONDERS

When the 1906 Chicago Cubs won the National League pennant, they did it in dominating fashion, winning 116 games, the most in major-league history. Across town, the Chicago White Sox earned their own pennant in the AL. But they did it in a completely different manner, seemingly despite their play. The "Hitless Wonders," as they came to be known, won 93 games that year while managing just 7 home runs and a .230 team batting average, the lowest in baseball. When the two teams faced off in the first and only all-Chicago World Series, the Cubs were heavily favored. But four games

into the best-of-seven series, despite the White Sox having committed eight errors and gotten only nine hits, the teams were tied at two games apiece. And then the series really turned upside-down. In the next two games, the White Sox sprayed 26 hits around the field, including 8 off of Hall of Fame pitcher Mordecai "Three Finger" Brown. Sox second baseman Frank Isbell hit four doubles in Game 5, and shortstop George Davis accounted for 10 runs in Games 5 and 6. The Hitless Wonders scored eight runs in each of those games to win the World Series and Chicago bragging rights.

land, and Buffalo, played one year as a minor-league team before becoming a major-league rival to the established National League (NL). Chicago won the pennant in that first minor-league season behind the pitching of Jack Katoll, who at one point tossed four straight shutouts.

When the AL made its official major-league start the next year, Chicago squared off in the league's first game against the Cleveland Blues on April 24, 1901, before 14,000 fans at the White Stockings' home field, the Cricket Club grounds. The team officially changed its name to the White Sox that day and beat the Blues 8–2. The Sox went on to win the first AL pennant. Pitcher Clark Griffith earned 24

CLARK GRIFFITH – Nicknamed "The Old Fox," Griffith was known for his baffling assortment of pitches. He spent eight superb seasons (1893–1900) with the Chicago Cubs before moving across town and leading the White Sox to the AL pennant.

CLARK GRIFFITH

victories on the mound and also managed the team. When Griffith left Chicago after the 1902 season, the role of pitching ace went to Guy "Doc" White, a dentist, violinist, and control pitcher who once went 36 consecutive innings without giving up a walk.

In 1903, the AL and NL began to face off at the end of each season in a championship series called the World Series. And in 1906, the Sox got their opportunity to take part. The south-side Chicago White Sox faced the north-side Chicago Cubs in a showdown for the ages. The Sox beat the heavily favored Cubs four games to two in the best-of-seven series on the strength of their pitching and clutch hitting. Pitcher Ed Walsh won two games in the series with a miniscule 0.60 earned run average (ERA).

Soon, however, the team's lack of offense would prove too much to overcome. Walsh won 40 games in 1908, but an anemic offense produced only three home runs. The Sox sank in the standings until the roster was rebuilt starting around 1914. That year, pitcher Urban "Red" Faber came to town. A spitballer with good control, Faber once tossed a mere 67 pitches in a full nine-inning game. Also new to the roster were right fielder "Shoeless" Joe Jackson, second baseman Eddie Collins, and pitcher Ed Cicotte.

The Sox reached the World Series in 1917 after a 100–54 season, then topped the New York Giants to win the world championship. They roared back to the World Series just two years later but were upset by the Cincin-

PITCHER · ED WALSH

As a young man, "Big Ed" Walsh worked in a Pennsylvania coal mine, where he developed great arm and shoulder strength. He joined the big leagues with nothing but that strong arm and a fastball. On team road trips, he roomed with spitballer Elmer Stricklett, who taught Walsh his craft. Once Walsh mastered the spitball, he mastered major-league hitters—inning after inning until he overworked his arm and could pitch no more. In 1908, Walsh pitched 464 innings, a modern record. He won 40 games while throwing 42 complete games that year—both White Sox feats that have never been duplicated.

STATS

White Sox seasons: 1904–16

Height: 6-1

Weight: 193

- 1.82 career ERA

- 2,964 career innings pitched

- 5-time AL leader in games pitched

- Baseball Hall of Fame inductee (1946)

ED WALSH
PITCHER

JOE JACKSON

nati Reds in eight games (in an experimental nine-game series). A year later, it would come to light that eight of Chicago's players had thrown the game, or lost on purpose in exchange for money. The eight would become known as the "Black Sox" for their misdeed. A young fan was reported to have asked Jackson, one of the Black Sox, "Say it ain't so, Joe." But it was so, and the franchise that had risen so high in baseball's early years would need decades to rebuild. Chicago had been burned again.

SHADOW OF THE BLACK SOX

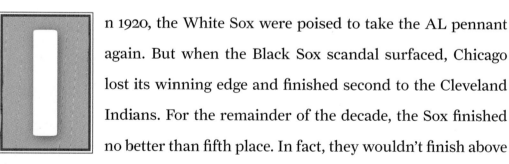n 1920, the White Sox were poised to take the AL pennant again. But when the Black Sox scandal surfaced, Chicago lost its winning edge and finished second to the Cleveland Indians. For the remainder of the decade, the Sox finished no better than fifth place. In fact, they wouldn't finish above third place for more than 30 years.

Still, the 1920s had its bright spots. Sure-handed Eddie Collins anchored the infield until 1926. Collins was a strong contact hitter, skilled at hit-and-run plays and laying down bunts, and he ran the bases with speed and smarts.

CATCHER > **CARLTON FISK**

In his first game for the Chicago White Sox, Carlton "Pudge" Fisk smashed a three-run homer against his former team, the Boston Red Sox. Fisk swung an uncommonly powerful bat for a catcher and, for a time, owned the White Sox career home run record as well as the major-league home run record for catchers. But Fisk's greatest strengths were his work ethic and durability; he managed to play a record 2,226 games at baseball's toughest position despite suffering numerous leg injuries. Fisk played until age 45, spending 13 of his 24 major-league seasons with Chicago.

STATS

White Sox seasons: 1981-93

Height: 6-2

Weight: 220

• Caught 2,226 games

• 1972 AL Rookie of the Year

• 376 career HR

• 11-time All-Star

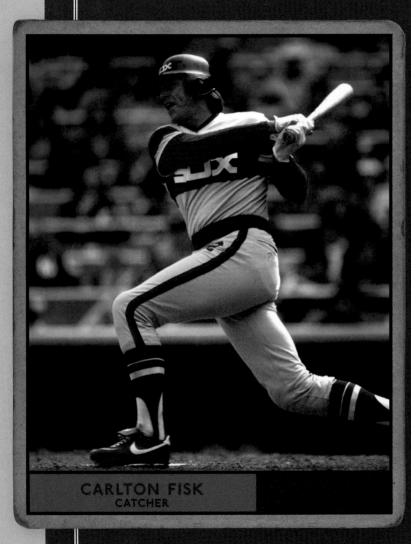

CARLTON FISK
CATCHER

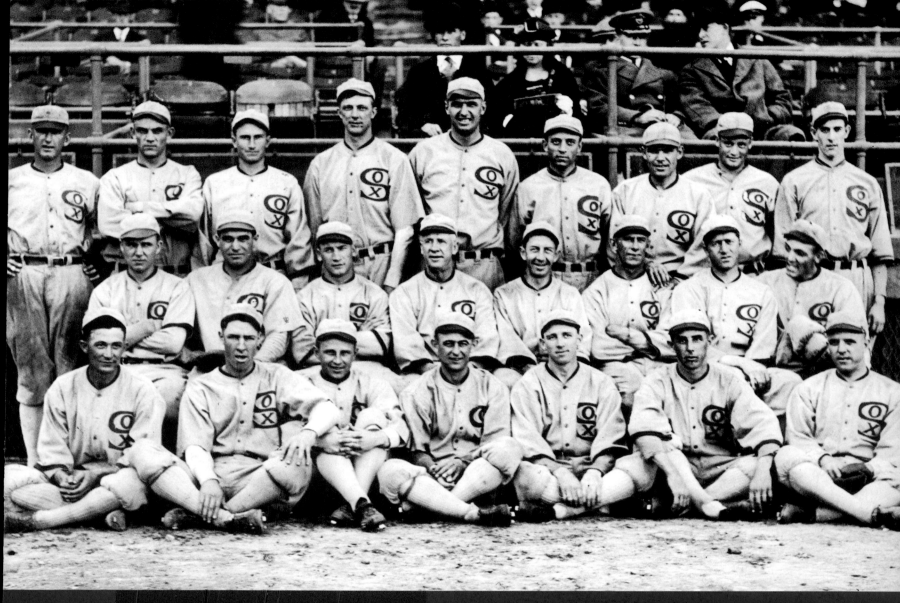

THE BLACK SOX SCANDAL

In Game 1 of the 1919 World Series, Chicago pitcher Ed Cicotte hit Cincinnati Reds second baseman Morrie Rath in the back with his second pitch of the game. Fans were stunned, as Cicotte was not a wild pitcher; the 29-game winner had hit only two batters all season. No, the pitch went exactly where Cicotte intended. Few knew it yet, but it was a signal: the fix was in. The White Sox were heavily favored to beat the Reds, but as the first game neared, rumors circulated that gamblers had paid a number of Chicago's players to let Cincinnati win. Cicotte's beaning of Rath let the gamblers know that the players had agreed to split the $100,000 bribe. The

"throw" was subtle—consisting of wild pitches, fielding errors, strikeouts, and a lack of hustle—and despite the rumors, no one was sure if the Sox had intentionally lost or if the Reds had simply been the better team. But in September 1920, pressured by investigators, Cicotte and outfielder Joe Jackson confessed. The eight players involved—Cicotte, Jackson, pitcher Lefty Williams, outfielder Happy Felsch, third baseman Buck Weaver, first baseman Chick Gandil, shortstop Swede Risberg, and third baseman Fred McMullin—were banned from baseball for life and became known forever thereafter as the Chicago "Black Sox."

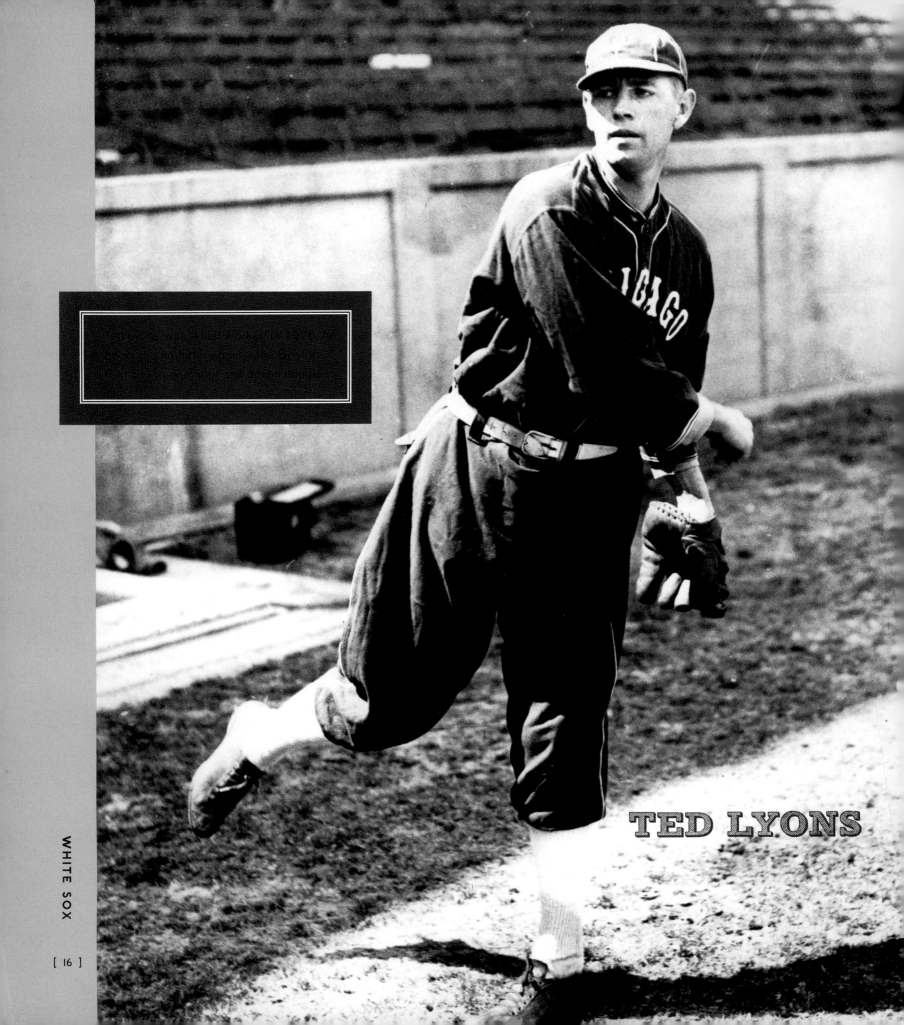

Ted Lyons was a fast worker. In 1926, he
pitched a no-hitter against the Boston
Red Sox in one hour and seven minutes.

TED LYONS

Another highlight was the emergence of pitcher Ted Lyons, who played at Baylor University in Texas when the Sox came to town in 1923 for spring training. Chicago invited Baylor to have its best pitcher throw against the Sox during a practice game. Lyons got the nod and knocked the Sox's socks off. He graduated that year, joined the team in July, and remained with the White Sox until he retired in 1942.

Lyons was the definition of durability, once pitching all 21 innings of a single extra-innings game. In 1931, he strained his arm, slowing his fastball, so he developed a knuckleball. Toward the end of the decade, he began to struggle again until player/manager Jimmie Dykes started pitching him only on Sundays. The Sox sold it as "Sundays with Lyons," and it was a huge draw at the gate. During his 21 years with Chicago, Lyons became the winningest pitcher in team history, amassing 260 victories.

Throughout the 1930s, Sox fans also gathered to cheer on Luke Appling. The young shortstop joined Chicago in 1930 but was slow to mature as a player, often booting easy ground balls, uncorking errant throws, and swinging wildly for the fences. But Appling developed into an able fielder and one of the league's most consistent batsmen. He became an adroit slap hitter, taking advantage of gaps in the spacious Comiskey Park outfield.

Appling and Lyons faced the difficult task of bringing the White Sox back to prominence—a task they would never accomplish. In seven seasons during the 1930s, the White Sox finished with a losing record. In 1932, they went an abysmal 49–102. The closest they came to success was in 1936 and 1937, with two third-place finishes in the eight-team AL. Not surprisingly, 1936 was Appling's greatest year, as he hit .388. Another star that season was first baseman Henry "Zeke" Bonura, who contributed 138 runs batted in (RBI). Bonura had a unique approach to fielding. If the ball looked too difficult to catch or scoop up, he watched it go by. One year, he avoided tough plays so fervently that he actually led the league in fielding percentage.

By 1938, Chicago was back in the AL cellar, and things didn't get much better during the 1940s. "The whole White Sox squad is up for trade," Dykes quipped during one especially poor season. "We'll trade anybody, everybody . . . if we can." The Sox produced only three winning seasons for the second straight decade, despite Appling's fine play. Then, in 1948, general manager Frank Lane arrived, aglow with new ideas to lead the White Sox out from the dark shadow of their past.

FIRST BASEMAN · FRANK THOMAS

Frank Thomas led the White Sox resurgence that began in the early '90s and culminated in a 2005 World Series crown. Dubbed "The Big Hurt" for his punishment of opposing pitchers, Thomas was arguably the greatest White Sox hitter ever. He set career club records in 11 offensive categories, including home runs, runs, total bases, and RBI. He relied not only on the strength of his hulking frame, but also on a sharp eye and patience. Thomas spent most of 2005 on the disabled list, but it was fitting that he was part of the world championship team during his final Chicago season.

STATS

White Sox seasons: 1990–2005

Height: 6-5

Weight: 250

• 5 seasons with 40 or more HR

• .305 career BA

• 2-time AL MVP

• 5-time All-Star

FRANK THOMAS
FIRST BASEMAN

THE SOX GET GO-GOING

The Chicago White Sox of the 1950s were known as the "Go-Go Sox" for their speed on the base paths and their hustle on defense. The team led the AL in stolen bases for 10 straight seasons starting in 1951. But the nickname could just as easily have come from the way the team was built. Under the direction of "Trader Lane," players came and went so rapidly that the team that started the 1951 season featured not a single player from the 1949 squad.

One noteworthy addition was second baseman Jacob "Nellie" Fox, who arrived in 1950 and played for the Sox until 1963, winning four AL batting titles and a Most Valuable Player (MVP) award along the way. Fox was one of baseball's all-time steadiest players. He almost never struck out, held the major-league fielding percentage record in his day, and once played 798 consecutive games at second base.

Another Sox great, left fielder Orestes "Minnie" Minoso, joined the team in 1951. Minoso was the first African American player to compete for Chicago and quickly became a White Sox fan favorite due to his enthusiastic play. Still, there were baseball fans who did not appreciate Minoso's presence. In 1953, he and pitcher Connie Johnson were forced to skip an exhibition game in Memphis, Tennessee, because a town ordinance prohibited blacks and

COMISKEY PARK

In 1908, White Sox owner Charlie Comiskey bought 15 acres of land at the corner of 35th Street and Shields Avenue on Chicago's working-class south side. Two years later, Comiskey Park, a $500,000 concrete-and-steel stadium, was complete. It held 35,000 fans, including 16,000 on wooden bleachers. The outfield stretched 420 feet deep to center and 362 feet down the lines. The first game was played there on July 1, 1910, against the St. Louis Browns. In July 1933, Major League Baseball's first All-Star Game was played there. Chicago outfielder Al Simmons and third baseman Jimmie Dykes played in the game, along with such

baseball legends as Babe Ruth, Jimmie Foxx, and Lefty Grove. Comiskey also hosted All-Star Games in 1950 and 1984. And from 1933 to 1950, the Negro League All-Star Game was played there as well. On September 30, 1990, when the last game was played at Comiskey Park, it was the oldest stadium in use—older than Boston's Fenway Park and Chicago's Wrigley Field. A new Comiskey Park was built directly across the road, and for a time, before old Comiskey was torn down, a person could stroll down 35th Street between the old Comiskey and the new.

SECOND BASEMAN · EDDIE COLLINS

Eddie Collins began his professional baseball career as a junior at Columbia University. Although college athletes were not allowed to play pro sports, Collins used a fake name and joined the Philadelphia Athletics—until his true identity was discovered. Eventually, Collins became one of the greatest second basemen ever. His quickness made him one of the earliest elite base stealers, and at the plate, Collins had few peers, maintaining a .333 average over 25 big-league seasons. For 12 of those seasons, he played for Chicago, including the 1917 world championship squad and 1919 "Black Sox" team.

STATS

White Sox seasons: 1915–26

Height: 5-9

Weight: 175

- .969 career fielding percentage
- 1914 AL MVP
- 744 career stolen bases
- Baseball Hall of Fame inductee (1939)

EDDIE COLLINS
SECOND BASEMAN

NELLIE FOX

Nellie Fox played bigger than his 160-
pound frame, leading the AL in singles
every season from 1954 to 1960.

WHITE SOX

THE COMISKEY FAMILY

Charlie Comiskey brought the White Sox to Chicago. Yet many people believe he also caused the Black Sox scandal. His teams were poorly paid compared with other clubs, leaving his players desperate for money. Comiskey's blame for the scandal is debatable. But what's not debatable is that the Comiskey family spent nearly 40 years trying to return the team to its pre-Black Sox glory. When Comiskey died in 1931, he left the Sox to his son, J. Louis Comiskey. The younger Comiskey brought in star players such as outfielder Al Simmons and third baseman Jimmie Dykes and established a minor-league farm system, but the highest the Sox ever finished under his leadership was third place. When he died in 1939, his wife, Grace Comiskey, took control. She maintained ownership until her death in 1956, at which time her children—Chuck Comiskey and Dorothy Rigney—took ownership. When Rigney sold her 54 percent of the team in 1958, the White Sox were no longer under Comiskey control, although Chuck, who still owned 46 percent, stayed on as executive vice president. But when he sold his share of the team in 1961, the Comiskey-Sox connection was broken. Under 60 years of Comiskey ownership, Chicago won five AL pennants and two World Series.

whites from playing together on the local field.

Another player who got the Sox going was center fielder "Jungle" Jim Rivera, who was known for his wild, belly-flopping slides and wilder personality. He once slid head-first into home plate—after slugging a home run into the outfield seats. When he emerged from the dust, he asked the photographers if they got their shot.

Pitcher Billy Pierce, meanwhile, led Chicago's efforts on the mound. With a hard fastball and a sharp, darting slider, Pierce relentlessly whipped baseballs past helpless hitters. Lane once said of the Go-Go's ace, "You didn't need a relief pitcher when he pitched. If he had a one-run lead going into the seventh or eighth inning, the ballgame was over."

With this hard-charging style of play, Chicago started winning. But after finishing third behind the New York Yankees and Cleveland Indians for five straight years, the Sox knew they still lacked pieces to the pennant puzzle. In 1957, they lured manager Al Lopez away from the Indians. They also added speedy outfielder Jim Landis and speedier shortstop Luis Aparicio, who became the premier base stealer on a team of base stealers. Aparicio combined with Fox to create one of the most exciting middle-infield combinations in baseball.

Under Lopez's direction, the Sox broke into second place in 1957 and 1958. And in 1959, led by hard-throwing pitcher Early Wynn, the Sox took over first

EARLY WYNN – Wynn (left) was all business as soon as he stepped onto the field, taking his job so seriously that he referred to the pitching mound as his "office." The star hurler could also hit and is one of only five big-league pitchers ever to slug a grand slam.

place in July and never gave it up. On September 22, the White Sox clinched their first pennant in 40 years—the first since the 1919 Black Sox had won it.

This time, Chicago gave its all in the World Series. Fox batted .375, while Aparicio hit .308. The White Sox rolled in Game 1 but could not get past the Los Angeles Dodgers, losing four games to two. "When we won the first game 11–0, I figured, 'Boy, this is going to be it,'" Pierce said later. "It didn't turn out that way, but I still think we had a great ballclub." The White Sox would have to wait another 40-plus years to reach the World Series again.

Playing every inning of his career at shortstop, Luis Aparicio won 9 Gold Glove awards and was a 10-time All-Star.

LUIS APARICIO

THIRD BASEMAN · ROBIN VENTURA

Robin Ventura came to the major leagues with big expectations after a stellar college career at Oklahoma State University and a stint with the 1988 U.S. Olympic team. Ventura met those expectations, and then some. He played 10 of his 16 major league seasons with the White Sox, and built a career on strong all-around play. He manned the "hot corner" with a sure glove, quick reflexes, and a strong arm. At the plate, his strength was driving runners home. In 1991, he knocked in 100 runs for the White Sox. And in 1996, he drove in 105.

STATS

White Sox seasons: 1989–98

Height: 6-1

Weight: 198

- Baseball America's College Player of the Decade (1980s)

- 1,182 career RBI

- 6-time Gold Glove winner

- 2 grand slams in a single game (1995)

ROBIN VENTURA
THIRD BASEMAN

NORTH AND SOUTH

or the next three decades, the White Sox would go "north and south" frequently—not on the map, but in the standings. The Sox played some exciting baseball but lacked consistency from year to year. Unlike the Go-Go Sox teams, which progressed steadily to the top of the league, the Sox of the 1960s, '70s, and '80s often found themselves in second place one season and fourth or fifth the next.

Following the successful 1959 season, the Sox floundered, dropping to fifth place by 1962. Again, a new squad was assembled, this one including pitchers Gary Peters and Hoyt Wilhelm. Peters won a total of 39 games in 1963 and 1964, while Wilhelm collected 98 saves for Chicago on his way to the Baseball Hall of Fame.

The 1964 White Sox finished the season with nine straight victories but fell one game short of the AL pennant. After another strong finish in 1965, they steadily declined, dropping to ninth place by 1968. Then, the 1970 White Sox team made a southward plunge like no other. They lost 106 games, a club record, and finished 42 games behind the first-place Minnesota Twins.

The White Sox enjoyed some fine achievements in the 1970s—just not in

WINNING UGLY

The 1983 White Sox got off to a slow start. Near the end of May, their record was a mere 16–24, and at the midseason All-Star break, they were just 40–37. Fortunately for the Sox, no team was dominating Chicago's division, the AL West. The Texas Rangers led at the break with a 44–34 record, three and a half games ahead of the Sox. But as Chicago began to pick up steam, Rangers manager Doug Rader was quoted in a Dallas newspaper as saying that the Sox weren't for real. "Their bubble has got to burst," he said. "They're not playing that well. They're winning ugly." The Sox used

Rader's quote as fuel for their charge to the playoffs. "Winning ugly" became the team's battle cry for the rest of the season, which the White Sox dominated. They went on five winning streaks of four games or more—the longest being an eight-game tear in mid-September. Chicago pummeled opponents that last stretch of the season, collecting nearly half of their AL-best 99 victories in August and September. By the end of the year, they were in the playoffs for the first time in 24 years, finishing an astonishing 22 games ahead of the third-place Rangers.

WHITE SOX

SHORTSTOP — LUKE APPLING

Luke Appling was famous for his ability to foul off pitch after pitch until he got one he liked. He once smacked away 17 foul balls in a single at-bat before ripping a triple. Appling approached his career much the same way. Although he never won a pennant with the luckless White Sox, he played all 20 of his big-league seasons with the team, perhaps waiting for the big season that never came. Even as his long career came to an end, Appling's hitting prowess barely diminished. In 1949, his 19th season, the 42-year-old hit .301 with 121 walks.

STATS

White Sox seasons: 1930–50

Height: 5-10

Weight: 183

* 7-time All-Star
* 2-time AL leader in BA
* .310 career BA
* Baseball Hall of Fame inductee (1964)

LUKE APPLING
SHORTSTOP

the win-loss column. Third baseman Bill Melton became the first Sox player to win the AL home run title with 33 blasts in 1971, and first baseman Dick Allen led the league with 37 home runs and 113 RBI to win AL MVP honors the very next year. Chicago rested much of its hopes on Allen, who joined the team after tumultuous seasons with the Philadelphia Phillies and St. Louis Cardinals. The first baseman drew fans to the park with his exciting combination of speed and power; during one 1972 game against the Minnesota Twins, he hit two inside-the-park home runs. Unfortunately, Allen's desire to play wasn't as great as his ability. The moody star quit the team with one month left in the 1974 season, despite leading the AL in home runs.

If Allen's decision was baffling to some, so were Wilbur Wood's knuckleballs to opposing batters. The left-handed Wood won 90 games between 1971 and 1974. And designated hitter Oscar Gamble put together a stellar season as part of a 1977 Sox team that became known as the "South Side Hitmen." The Hitmen slugged 192 home runs, the most ever by a White Sox team at the time. Gamble led the charge with 31 dingers, and outfielder Richie Zisk slammed 30 of his own. The team finished in third place but kept the fans' attention, drawing a team-record 1,657,135 spectators to Comiskey Park.

In 1983, the Sox jumped into first place in the AL Western Division (the league was split into two divisions in 1969) and drew more than two million fans. That team featured hard-nosed catcher Carlton Fisk, 24-game-winner

LEFT FIELDER · MINNIE MINOSO

Saturnino Orestes Arrieta "Minnie" Minoso was born in Cuba. At age 14, he quit school to work in the local sugar cane fields, and eventually, started a plantation ballclub, and his skills earned him a trip to Havana to play for the Ambro Cuba Mining Company team. He later joined the New York Cubans, the Cleveland Indians, and, finally, the Chicago White Sox. Minoso was a fan favorite due to his hustle and enthusiasm as a leader of the "Go-Go Sox." Sadly, Minoso was not on Chicago's pennant-winning 1959 team, as he was part of the 1958 trade that brought pitching ace Early Wynn to Chicago.

MINNIE MINOSO
LEFT FIELDER

Born: 1925

White Sox seasons: 1951-57, 1960-61, 1964, 1976, 1980

Height: 5-10

Weight: 175

• .298 career BA

• 7-time All-Star

• 3-time AL leader in stolen bases

• 3-time Gold Glove winner

CENTER FIELDER · JIM LANDIS

Jim Landis roamed Comiskey Park's center field with speed and grace for eight seasons. Yankees manager Casey Stengel once commented that Landis's defense cut triples down to doubles and doubles down to singles. The sure-gloved Landis positioned himself well, got good jumps on fly balls, and made strong throws. And while not known for his hitting, he did many little things right at the plate. He averaged 71 walks per season, and in 1959, he led the AL in sacrifice hits—bunts and fly outs that moved runners to the next base. He was also a skilled base stealer.

White Sox seasons: 1957–64

Height: 6-1

Weight: 180

· 1962 All-Star

· 5-time Gold Glove winner

· .989 career fielding percentage

· 50 career triples

JIM LANDIS
CENTER FIELDER

LaMarr Hoyt, and clutch-hitting outfielder Harold Baines. The number-one pick of the 1977 draft, Baines had been scouted by the White Sox since he was a Little-Leaguer and would go on to play three stints in Chicago during his big-league career.

The 1983 Sox finished with 99 victories, the most since their 1917 world championship team, and faced the Baltimore Orioles in the AL Championship Series (ALCS). They lost, three games to one, and never found such success again for the rest of the 1980s. Chicago would finish near the bottom of the league standings the rest of the decade.

RON KITTLE

RON KITTLE – Chicago's terrific 1983 season was made possible in part by Ron Kittle. Slugging 35 home runs and driving in 100 runs, the first-year outfielder captured both AL Rookie of the Year honors and a place on the AL All-Star team.

JACK McDOWELL — "Black Jack" played in a rock band outside of baseball and made noise on the mound with his fastball. He put together four great White Sox seasons in the early 1990s before injuries and hot-tempered behavior derailed his career.

A STEADY RISE

f the White Sox of the 1960s, '70s, and '80s shifted like a knuckleball, the Sox of the '90s and 2000s sped upward like a hard-rising fastball. For 15 years beginning in 1990, Chicago never finished lower than third place—and that low only three times.

In 1990, a youthful Chicago squad took the field, led by enormous first baseman Frank Thomas, third baseman Robin Ventura, and pitcher Jack McDowell. The team boasted speed, defense, power, enthusiasm—and some of the league's best players. In 1993, Thomas won the AL MVP award, and McDowell won the Cy Young Award as the league's best pitcher. That season, Chicago reached the playoffs for the first time in 10 years. The young White Sox met the veteran Toronto Blue Jays in the ALCS. Chicago battled hard, erasing a two-games-to-none deficit with a pair of victories in Toronto. But McDowell never found his best stuff, and the Sox never won a third game. The Jays took the pennant and went on to win their second straight world championship.

Chicago came back strong the next year, charging to a 67–46 mark, but a players' strike then cut the season short and cancelled the 1994 World

Series. The disruption seemed to kill Chicago's momentum, and the Sox would climb no higher than second place in the newly formed AL Central Division for the remainder of the decade.

At the start of the new millennium, the White Sox emerged as an offensive machine led by Thomas and slugging right fielder Magglio Ordoñez. During the 2000 season, five players scored more than 100 runs, four players hit over .300, five players knocked in more than 90 runs, and the Sox led the AL in runs scored. It was a slugfest all season long as the Sox collected an AL-best 95 victories. Excitement in the "Windy City" came to a screeching halt, though, as the Sox were swept by the Seattle Mariners in three tight playoff games.

The Sox hovered near the top of the AL Central for the next four years, and when they finally returned to the postseason in 2005, it was in surprising fashion. No player batted .300, no pitcher won 20 games, and only one player—first baseman Paul Konerko—knocked in 100 runs. Few people expected the White Sox to make the playoffs, even after the team got off to a blazing 24–7 start.

Former Sox shortstop-turned-manager Ozzie Guillen lit a fire under his squad and engineered a small-ball strategy that involved moving runners

RIGHT FIELDER · JOE JACKSON

"Shoeless Joe" Jackson's 13th major-league season was an unlucky one, as he was barred from major-league baseball for his role in throwing the 1919 World Series. But that stretch of 13 seasons was anything but unlucky for Shoeless Joe. A natural ballplayer, Jackson was a swift, strong-throwing outfielder and was even better as a hitter. The legendary Babe Ruth is said to have mimicked Jackson's batting stance. With a lifetime .356 average, Shoeless Joe may have been the best hitter never to win a batting title. During the 1919 World Series that Jackson supposedly threw, he batted .375 with six RBI.

STATS

White Sox seasons: 1915–20

Height: 6-1

Weight: 200

• 2-time AL leader in hits

• 168 career triples

• 1,772 career hits

• Career-high .408 BA in 1911

JOE JACKSON
RIGHT FIELDER

MANAGER · AL LOPEZ

As a player in the 1930s and '40s, Al Lopez was a catcher with a gift for handling pitchers. It was a gift that served him well when he moved into the managerial ranks. Lopez was not only skilled at handling players but also at making the most of their unique skills. As a coach for the Cleveland Indians, Lopez relied on power hitting and pitching. But when he became the White Sox's skipper in 1957, he preached a speed game that suited Comiskey's deep outfield and his players' natural abilities. Lopez engineered the "Go-Go Sox" and Chicago's first pennant in 40 years.

STATS

White Sox seasons as manager:
    1957–65, 1968–69

Height: 5-11

Weight: 165

Managerial Record: 840–650

AL Pennant: 1959

AL LOPEZ
MANAGER

home one base at a time. Outstanding defense by such players as catcher A.J. Pierzynski and a strong pitching staff led by Jon Garland kept the Sox in close games all year. The Sox slumped badly at the start of August, and the Indians seemed poised to overtake them. But Chicago then caught a second wind and blew through the end of its schedule, sweeping the Indians in the season's final three games to win the AL Central, 99–63.

A.J. PIERZYNSKI – Few players got under opponents' skin like Pierzynski. But while many opponents disliked him for his cocky actions, Sox fans loved him for his tough defensive play and a sharp batting eye that made him almost impossible to strike out.

JOE CREDE

Third baseman Joe Crede's sure glove
and increasingly powerful bat made him
a rising star on Chicago's south side.

From then on, the Sox were unstoppable. In the face of an 88-year world championship drought, and still in the far-reaching shadow of the Black Sox scandal, Chicago dominated the postseason, winning an incredible 11 of 12 games. Young third baseman Joe Crede and outfielder Jermaine Dye starred as Chicago mowed down the Boston Red Sox, Los Angeles Angels of Anaheim, and Houston Astros to become world champions. "It means a lot not only to us in the clubhouse but to the organization, to the fans, to the city, and it's just a great feeling," said Dye. "We're just happy to be able to bring a championship to the city."

With no intentions of waiting another 88 years for a fourth title, Chicago added powerful designated hitter Jim Thome to the roster before the 2006 season. There would be no repeat, however. Even though Thome slugged 42 home runs to help the 2006 Sox go 90–72, they finished third in the AL Central and out of the playoffs, leaving them eager to return to postseason glory in 2007.

The Chicago White Sox have taken their fans to the highest highs and lowest lows in their 11-decade history. Thanks to their beloved Sox, fans have known glory, despair, frustration, and—with their 2005 World Series triumph—redemption and jubilation. The Black Sox, decades of bad seasons, and numerous near-misses all seem faint memories as today's White Sox try to find a permanent place atop the AL.

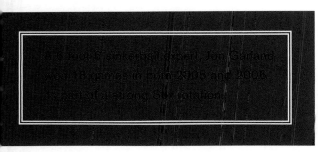

A's not a sinkerball expert, Jon Garland won 18 games in both 2005 and 2006 as part of a strong Sox rotation.

Allen, Dick 32

All-Star Game 21

AL batting championships 20

AL Central Division championships 38, 43

AL Championship Series 35, 37

AL pennants 9, 13, 24, 27, 29, 42

Aparicio, Luis 25, 27

Appling, Luke 17, 18, 31

Baines, Harold 35

Baseball Hall of Fame 8, 11, 22, 29, 31

"Black Sox" 13, 15, 22, 24, 27, 47

Blum, Geoff 40

Bonura, Henry 18

Cicotte, Ed 10, 15

Collins, Eddie 10, 13, 22

Comiskey, Charlie 6, 21, 24

Comiskey Park 17, 21, 32, 34, 42

Crede, Joe 47

Cricket Club 9

Cy Young Award 37

Davis, George 8

Dye, Jermaine 5, 47

Dykes, Jimmie 17, 18, 21, 24

Faber, Urban 10

Felsch, Happy 15

first season 9

Fisk, Carlton 14, 32

Fox, Nellie 20, 25, 27

Gamble, Oscar 32

Gandil, Chick 15

Garland, Jon 43

Gold Glove award 28, 33, 34

Griffith, Clark 9–10

Guillen, Ozzie 38

Harris, Willie 5

Hoyt, LaMarr 35

Isbell, Frank 8

Jackson, Joe 10, 13, 15, 39

Johnson, Connie 20

Konerko, Paul 38

Landis, Jim 25, 34

Lane, Frank "Trader" 18, 20, 25

Lopez, Al 25, 42

Lyons, Ted 17, 18

major-league records 8, 11, 14

McDowell, Jack 37

McMullin, Fred 15

Melton, Bill 32

Minoso, Minnie 20, 33

MVP award 19, 20, 22, 32, 37

Ordoñez, Magglio 38

Peters, Gary 29

Pierce, Billy 25, 27

Pierzynski, A.J. 43

Podsednik, Scott 40

Risberg, Swede 15

Rivera, Jim 25

Rookie of the Year award 14

Simmons, Al 21, 24

Stricklett, Elmer 11

team records 11, 14, 29

Thomas, Frank 19, 37, 38

Thome, Jim 47

Ventura, Robin 28, 37

Walsh, Ed 10, 11

Weaver, Buck 15

White, Guy 10

Wilhelm, Hoyt 29

Williams, Lefty 15

Wood, Wilbur 32

world championships 5, 10, 19, 22, 35, 40, 47

World Series 5, 8, 10, 13, 15, 24, 27, 38, 39, 40, 47

World Series records 40

Wynn, Early 25, 33

Zisk, Richie 32